10/13/

DUGOUTS, ICONS AND DREAMS

MINOR LEAGUE BASEBALL CAREER, MAJOR LEAGUE BASEBALL MEMORIES

BILL DAVIDSON

Bill J Davidson

Wasteland Press

www.wastelandpress.net
Shelbyville, KY USA

Dugouts, Icons and Dreams:
Minor League Baseball Career,
Major League Baseball Memories
by Bill Davidson

First Printing – April 2018
ISBN: 978-1-68111-226-8
Library of Congress Control Number: 2018935622

Printed in the U.S.A.

0   1   2   3   4   5   6   7

To my father, Howard:
A great athlete and a great role model

ACKNOWLEDGMENTS

Family ties are important in all our endeavors. My parents, now deceased, always stressed the importance of family. My three sisters—Jane, Trudy, Kathy—and I remain close to this day. I'm very proud of my two sons, Will and Ben. Will, an engineer, lives in Asheville, North Carolina, and is engaged to April. We visit each other often. Ben, a schoolteacher, lives in Denver, Colorado, with his wife Karen and two children, Kyla and Evan. We also visit each other whenever possible.

My wife Ellen has helped me immeasurably with this book project. Ellen, a former schoolteacher (English, French, and Spanish), has been a valuable source of information. This is the second marriage for both of us. We dated in our younger years, went our separate ways, reunited, and recently celebrated our sixteenth anniversary. Ellen has three children—Kim Nave, Niki Mercado, and Ted Page. Kim lives in Lumberton, New Jersey, with her husband Paul and their two sons, Paul and Alex. Niki lives in Cherry Hill, New Jersey, with her husband Wilson. Ted, a great athlete in high school and Boston College, lives in Wyomissing, Pennsylvania. Ted played football at Boston College (defensive tackle) under coach Tom Coughlin, former New York Giants head coach. A knee injury prevented any professional aspirations.

Unlike my children, Ellen's children live nearby, ensuring frequent contact. Both of our families get together on occasion and the camaraderie is very gratifying. It reinforces the value of family ties.

Writing a book has proved to be a lot of work, research, and fun. Words of encouragement are always appreciated. "How's your book coming along?" "Can't wait to read your book." So, in addition to my family members, I would like to acknowledge those who expressed their interest. Special thanks to Richard Pisani for his help and computer expertise. Saul N. Miller, DDS, offered insightful quotes. Thanks also to B. J. Ward for his encouragement and advice.

All those on the following list offered positive remarks: Bob Viggiano, Al Harris, Gary Morrison, Jim Draper, Ron Rossi, Gino Massimi, Bob Nutt, Bob Ward, Bob Gini, Sharon McDermott, Bob and Denise O'Donnell, Jimmy and Meg O'Donnell, Billy Wagner, Bill Kurdyla, Ron Kashon, Rocky Iacovone, Andy Taormina, and Brian Feldschneider, Golden Pheasant Golf Club Pro.

Special thanks to my editor, Susan Giffin. She guided me through the entire process. Being a complete novice in the book publishing business, I appreciate publisher Tim Renfrow, who showed great patience in responding to my "rookie" inquiries. His advice and expertise has made me glad I chose Wasteland Press.

CONTENTS

Spring Training

Preface! Prologue! Introduction! A typical book normally has one of these introductory sections. In keeping with the central theme of the book—baseball and dreams—I chose Spring Training instead.

In baseball, spring training conjures up many clichés: *Hope springs eternal. Forever young, start from scratch,* to mention a few. Spring training was always a fun time in my career. It was a time to start over, work on weaknesses, and make other improvements without the pressure that the coming season would bring. In my eleven-year career, ten springs were spent in Florida and one in California. Coming from winters in New Jersey, I welcomed the warm February and March temperatures. It was the perfect setting to cultivate my dreams.

After hearing some of my unique experiences in baseball, friends often suggested that I write a book. "Heart of Gold," a DVD by Neil

Young, showcases one of his concerts, which took place in historic Ryman Auditorium in Nashville, Tennessee, site of the original Grand Ole Opry. He opened with a song, "It's a Dream."

The lyrics inspired me to record my memories before they fade away. As I will divulge later in the book, this same Ryman Auditorium provided an unforgettable personal experience.

TOP OF THE FIRST INNING:

Dreams

Most professional athletes acknowledge that their accomplishments were the realization of childhood dreams. Like most youngsters, I had these dreams. My father was a sports enthusiast and always encouraged me in my athletic endeavors, without any pushing or pressure whatsoever.

With my own two sons, I always tried to let them develop their own interests. I encouraged them in their sports ventures, not wanting them to measure their accomplishments against my success. I enjoyed watching them participate in baseball, basketball, football, and golf. I think the lack of pressure led to their enjoyment of sports and the opportunity to pursue their own dreams.

My father was a great athlete. He was short—5 feet 6 inches. I heard that he was very fast. Once, when we were discussing bunting, he told me an incredible story. He once went 5 for 5 in a game, ALL

BUNTS. I said, "On the third one, weren't they playing you for a bunt?" He said it didn't matter, he just placed it past them. He was a great role model. He would stop whatever he was doing if I asked him to have a catch or hit me some grounders.

Perhaps one of our family stories was the best indication that being a ballplayer was my destiny. My father was sitting on the front step, waiting for someone to pick him up for a ball game. My mother was also sitting on the step, waiting for someone to take her to the hospital. She was expecting a child. I was born in the seventh inning!

Playing in youth baseball, football, basketball, and track programs improved my skills. By junior high school, my dreams intensified. Looking back, I was fortunate to have had parents who also stressed the importance of academics. This was important in those pre-high school years. Fulfillment of dreams requires a strong foundation. In high school, I played baseball, basketball, and track. Although basketball was my favorite sport, baseball and the major leagues was my *ultimate* dream.

As a youngster, perhaps since sixth grade, I always dreamed of becoming a professional baseball player. I was fortunate enough to have had the necessary athletic talent to make that dream a reality. I enjoyed an eleven-year career, coming up just short of the major leagues. However, for the longest time, I felt that I had not achieved my goal.

At a concert of the great singer and composer, Paul Anka, I heard him make a statement prior to performing one of his songs. It provoked some thought. "As a composer, every song that you write doesn't have to be a hit to give you pleasure." It is my hope that any aspiring youngster with dreams will realize, as I have, that while the goal may not be achieved, the pursuit of that dream is equally as important.

My dentist, Saul N. Miller, DDS, is a very introspective person who shared his own personal quote on excellence and perfection: "Strive for excellence; you will get closer to perfection. Strive for perfection; you will never be satisfied."

B. J. Ward is an award-winning poet from New Jersey, who has compared baseball players with poets. I have had the pleasure of attending several of his readings. Ward says, "Baseball players, like poets, need to be comfortable with uncertainty, with the living in the moment but also with strategy, planning, the length of line and a poem, a game, and a season." So true! He also uses a great analogy: "A poet sitting down at his or her desk doesn't know this will be the day of writing their greatest work—just like a ballplayer plodding through a 162-game season doesn't know this will be the day of a great accomplishment."

Victor Cheng, founder of Case Interview and author of *Chasing Dreams*, says, "The pursuit of a dream irrespective of likelihood of success has intrinsic value separate from the outcome."

I hope that my experiences in baseball will provide reading enjoyment and a different perspective on dream fulfillment and pursuit.

BOTTOM OF THE FIRST:
High School

In high school, I was fortunate to have good coaches, enabling me to further my skill level. Basketball became my favorite sport; however, baseball was the vehicle to help me achieve my dream.

I also participated in track, a carryover from my younger years. My parents were involved in a fraternal insurance group called the Artisans. Each year, a regional track meet was held in Ocean City, New Jersey. Relay races, sprints, and so on were featured, including my favorite, the long jump. This presented a dilemma: baseball and track occurred in the same season. Unlike the present era when one cannot play both sports, I managed to do both, much to the dismay of my baseball coach. He thought it would affect my baseball performance. "You know, you had an error last week," he'd remind me. My track coach somehow scheduled the long jump early in the track meet. Since the baseball game was starting within the hour, there was little time to change. This led to the unusual sight of a long jumper performing in a baseball suit. It all worked out. I was undefeated and won the state championship, with a leap of over 21 feet!

High school basketball was a very popular sport in our area, and it provided lasting memories. I attended Woodrow Wilson, in Camden, New Jersey. Four teams—Wilson, Camden Catholic, Camden, and St. Joseph's—competed in a City Series format. Competition was strong, with players from the same neighborhood striving for *bragging rights*. Winning the City Series was almost comparable to winning the state championship. Crowds were enormous in the local Armory Arena.

Numerous major league organizations recruited me for baseball. After high school graduation, I attended many baseball tryout camps in the area. Major league organizations conducted these camps where standout performers received contract offers. Playing baseball in various independent leagues, with major league scouts in attendance, brought my dream closer to reality. I received many professional baseball offers in addition to college scholarships. My love of basketball probably kept me from signing a professional baseball contract, however.

Temple University in Philadelphia, Pennsylvania, offered a scholarship for baseball and basketball. I accepted. In so doing, I put my baseball dream on hold.

CITY SERIES CHAMPS: *The 1955 Woodrow Wilson team that won the City Series basketball championship included: kneeling, l. to r., Bill Shaw, Ernie Trebing, Sam Croge, Bill Davidson and Jack Vane.*

Back row, Dave Andrus, Vince Dorczuk, Don Stewart, Coach Pete Mussa, Paul Jelus, Joe Cordner and Bill Burcat

TOP OF THE SECOND:
College/Yankee Stadium

Temple University gave me my first introduction to icons that would permeate my future athletic career. Basketball coach and future Hall of Famer Harry Litwack and players like Guy Rodgers—future hall of famer—and Hal Lear, an all-star performer, were class players. I feel blessed that my athletic ability enabled me to associate with these outstanding individuals. It enriched me as a person, as well as my career, business, and life in general.

In my opinion, Guy Rodgers and Hal Lear formed the best back court in college basketball...ever! Playing against them every day was a real basketball education. Rodgers was so quick; he could dribble the basketball from one end of the court faster than most people can run without a ball.

Lear had the "Big Three." This is a prime requisite for a great basketball player: outside shot, jumper, and drive. Indeed, Lear had all three. He was a better shooter than Rodgers. In one-on-one games, I could hold my own vs Rodgers.

Lear was another story. His ultra-quick first step made guarding him closely a bad choice. Lear probably would have been a good NBA player. He played in the Eastern League, choosing to stay in Philadelphia. Except for star players, salaries were low in the late 50s and early 60s.

After my freshman year, I faced a difficult decision. The New York Yankees invited me to a three-day workout at Yankee Stadium. Working out with icons, such as Mickey Mantle, Phil Rizzuto, Yogi Berra, Whitey Ford, Tony Kubek, and Bobby Richardson, coaches Frank Crosetti and Bill Dickey, and manager Casey Stengel, was an overwhelming experience.

Should I give up my favorite sport, basketball and the prestigious Big Five—one of the nation's best—or commit to the Yankees? The Big Five was a basketball conference born in the 1950s. Five Philadelphia-area schools: Temple University, University of Pennsylvania, Villanova University, St. Joseph's College, and La Salle College joined the conference. They played all games in the historic Palestra, which was the University of Pennsylvania's home court. It was a huge success. All games sold out. Coming from the same area, many players were familiar with each other's ability. This produced fierce competition. Many players played with or against each other in high school, or neighborhood teams. Spirit was high. Tradition was born. Bands from rival schools performed. They flew banners and traded insults. Occasionally, doubleheaders were on the schedule. The Palestra held about 9,500 spectators, and the noise level was incredible. All of this made my decision to turn professional extremely difficult.

Unfortunately, colleges had a freshman rule in effect during this period: freshmen could not play on the varsity team. Fortunately, Temple had a freshman team. This allowed me at least to enjoy the competition provided by the Big Five freshman teams, which took place at the Palestra. We also traveled occasionally with the varsity.

One trip to the U.S. Naval Academy was enjoyable. We stayed in the barracks and ate in the mess hall. My teammate and friend, Joey Goldenberg, played the next three years on the varsity squad. In later years, Joey was a very successful basketball coach at West Philadelphia High School. Joey was also inducted into the prestigious Jewish Basketball Hall of Fame.

Our schedule ended before the varsity, and I felt the urge to play more basketball. I joined a team called Spike's Trophies, a well-known award store in Philadelphia. The owner was Spike Shandleman, who knew I had played at Temple. We played preliminary games at all the Philadelphia Warriors' (NBA) home games. It was enjoyable. Two standout players were Jim "Tee" Parham and Sonny Hill. Sonny became a radio and television sports personality. Since I loved to shoot and was considered a scorer, my only complaint was that there was only one basketball! I remember playing a game at a famous recreation center, located at 25th and Diamond in Philadelphia. My parents and I were the only white people in the gym. After the game, a spectator came up to my father and said, "That boy plays like a black boy." I considered it a high compliment.

Rather than wait three more years, I signed with the Yankees and achieved my goal to be a professional baseball player! I did, however, return to Temple in the baseball off-seasons to obtain my degree. Playing in the major leagues remained my goal. Ironically, a few years after I signed, a rule change took place. If someone signed a professional contract, he could now play another sport in college, other than the sport in which he became a professional. Under this rule, I could have played basketball in college. Too late for me, however, others have since taken advantage of the rule.

Hal Lear – Temple University – 1956

BOTTOM OF THE SECOND:
Yankee Rookie Camp/
Casey Stengel

My career began with a special rookie camp invitation, which took place in St. Petersburg, Florida. The camp overlapped the New York Yankees' spring training camp in 1957. All the players and coaches I mentioned in my tryout at Yankee Stadium were in attendance, including pitcher Don Larsen who had the perfect game win in the 1956 World Series. The camp was presided over by Casey Stengel. Casey was famous for his malaprops, much like Yogi Berra and his pithy quotes.

For a rookie, this camp was a memorable experience that lasts a lifetime. Working out, dining together at night, hanging out with Yankee stars (future Hall of Fame players), and sitting on the dining room porch and listening to Casey "holding court," were added bonuses. This was a great learning experience, and start for my career: learning how to play the "Yankee way."

Casey had a "Trip around the Bases" speech, which was both instructive and hilarious. Some players, who had previously heard it, could imitate it to perfection. Casey summoned all the players, "Let's go over to the dugout. Come on, I don't have all day. I have a luncheon to attend. What do you do in the dugout? You don't spit water on the guy next to you. You watch the pitcher. Look for patterns. Plan for your turn at bat. OK, over to the on-deck circle. You don't kneel there, figuring out your batting average. You're watching the opposition, planning your strategy. Check the outfielders. Is the right fielder left- or right-handed? This information can help you take an extra base, if the ball is hit on the opposite side of his glove hand.

"OK, over to first base." Here he did what he always did: intersperse instructions with bits of humor. He showed the proper lead and how a cross-over first step could save us a step and a half. "When running on a hit-and-run play, take a glance at the pitch. Don't run with your head down. These are good fields; there's no rocks on the base paths."

Moving on to second base, he demonstrated proper leads. Moving on to third base: walking lead on the foul side and return on the fair side, blocking the catcher's view. Casey said, "Tony Kubek got me many runs by turning his shoulder on a catcher's throw, thereby causing it to glance away from the third baseman."

Frank Crosetti, Yankee coach and infield instructor, was a stark contrast to Casey. I learned more from Frank at this camp than in my entire career. His instruction on double-play techniques was especially beneficial. He would say, "This is the way I did it. This is the way Willie Miranda (Yankee infielder) did it. I want you to develop your own style; however, there are some techniques that you must follow." He went on to highlight these techniques. For any baseball *enthusiasts* reading this book, I'll explain a few. Perhaps you will gain some insight into what the shortstop and second baseman are doing during the game. It may even provide more enjoyment as you're watching your favorite major league team. You will be able to pick out mistakes the players make. Even announcers will blame the wrong player on a given play.

Watch the shortstop or second baseman, whoever is the designated "captain," put his glove to his face, with a man on first. It's his way of telling his teammate covering second of a steal attempt. Open mouth means *you* cover, closed mouth signifies *me*. The pitcher will look at the shortstop or second baseman to see who will cover second on a ball hit back to the pitcher. The shortstop or second baseman will tap his chest, signifying that he will cover. You might ask why this is necessary. Well, unlike amateur baseball—high school, sandlot, and even college ball—professional baseball players rely on percentages. The shortstop and second baseman are looking at the catcher's signals to the pitcher.

For simplicity, let's say 1 is a fastball and 2 is a curve. In the high minor leagues, AA and AAA and the major leagues, the hitters and pitchers are at a higher skill level. Generally, a hitter will pull an off-speed pitch and hit the fast ball to the opposite field. Infielders know how the pitcher will pitch to a given hitter and know the hitter's tendencies. Therefore, just because a hitter is right-handed, doesn't mean the second baseman will cover second on a steal attempt. Does this always work? NO! However, *percentage* comes into play. Professional pitchers, especially at the higher levels, can pinpoint their pitches, and *percentage* wins out.

Getting back to the announcer's typical mistake, I'll provide a simple example. There's a man on first, one out, double play opportunity. Ball hit to the second baseman, shortstop covers second by favoring the right field side of the bag. Second baseman throws the ball to the right of the shortstop or infield side of the bag. Shortstop misses the throw. Announcer says, "Second baseman made a bad throw." WRONG! Had the shortstop approached the bag under control, ready to go left or right, not anticipating a certain area, the throw would have been perfect—chest high at the bag. Therefore, the shortstop was at fault, not the second baseman. Hopefully, you will become an informed critic and even enjoy the game more.

Another *mistake* that shortstops and second basemen make is called *reaching*. They reach for the ball on a double play opportunity, with the glove hand only, and bring the glove hand down to meet the throwing hand, and wind up to throw. These are wasted motions that can prevent making the double play. A time-saving technique would be to have your throwing hand close to your glove hand, "short-arming" the throw, instead of using a wind-up motion. With practice, a short-arm motion can produce surprising velocity. Yankee infield instructor Jerry Coleman would spot me at the breakfast buffet, and from his table, without looking up from his newspaper, he would casually remark, "You were reaching yesterday."

While I was still playing, I would return to my high school and give a mini clinic before leaving for spring training. In later years, one student, who is now deceased, was in our golf group. Alex Curcio said I was his "idol" and reminded me of the clinic. Before golf each week, we reviewed the mistakes that the local big-league team had made. It's incredible how many times the wrong player received the blame for those mistakes.

Later in my career, I was traded to other organizations. Players always made the above mistakes. I had to teach my new second base teammate the correct way to execute for the benefit of our team. This doesn't speak well of some infield instructors, both past and present, at the minor and major league level.

Casey's performance, along with Frank Crosetti's expert infield instructions, made for lasting impressions. In retrospect, it's not surprising the Yankees won so often, touching all the bases.

Casey Stengel

Stengel in 1953
Manager

NEW YORK YANKEES
SPRING TRAINING CAMP - 1956

Front Row,   *seated from left:*   3rd - **BILL DAVIDSON**

Middle Row,   *seated from left:*   2nd - *Bill Dickey, 3rd - Ralph Houk,*
                                          4th - Eddie Lopat, 5th - Casey Stengel,
                                          6th - Johnny Neun, 7th - Frank Crosetti

Back Row, standing from left: 1st - *Marv Thorneberry, 3rd - Tony Kubek,*
                                          4th - Deron Johnson

Yankee spring training – 1957

TOP OF THE THIRD:
Professional Debut/ Saner

My first assignment was Peoria, Illinois. Baseball in this period (1957) had Class D, C, B, A, AA, AAA, and major leagues. Peoria was Class B. Peoria was a small town and proved to be a perfect place for an apprenticeship. The league was called the Three I League: Illinois, Indiana, and Iowa. Some cities in the league included Peoria, Davenport, Keokuk, Burlington, Cedar Rapids, and Evansville.

Although my teammates and I were serious at game time, this lower level in the professional ladder to the big leagues provided a fun atmosphere. All of us were the best of our respective high schools and colleges and had the same dreams. Our skill level was high, but being young, we played pranks and games every day.

One "game" in particular between me and our first baseman, Jimmy Johnston, remains with me to this day. During batting practice or fielding ground balls and so on, we would ask, "Did you see that (any word)?" If you responded in any way by turning your head, for instance, and acknowledging the question, you lost. Or by asking, "What?" We kept a running total in the clubhouse, and for each loss, the player owed a Coke. Each win created great glee and fist pumping. I started inserting the word *saner* in my quest for victory.

To this day, I use it occasionally. If my wife misplaces something, I'm liable to ask, "Did you look in the *saner?*" If I had stayed in contact with Jimmy, I could call and perhaps *saner* him.

Our manager was Vern Hoscheit, a former major league player and coach. Vern was perfect for this level of professional baseball. He was somewhat of a father figure to all of us young players. We drove station wagons for travel since the cities weren't that far apart. This provided for some interesting conversations, not all of them about baseball.

One game that always remained with me occurred in Davenport, Iowa. I hit a ball down the right field foul line over the fence, which appeared to be a home run. The first base umpire signaled fair ball. I rounded first and heard the plate umpire yelling, "Foul ball." I wasn't happy. The ball really appeared fair, curving around the foul pole. Our entire team protested. I came back to the batter's box, and instead of getting ready to hit, I knelt off to the side and pretended to tie my shoe. I needed a minute to cool down. The umpire said, "Batter up." I continued tying my shoe. The umpire ordered the pitcher to pitch *without* me in the batter's box. The count on me was two balls and two strikes. I watched a *high* pitch cross the plate. The umpire yelled, "Strike!" It was strike three. I went from a home run to a strike out. I argued, and the umpire threw me out of the game. All our bench players were banished to the clubhouse, except for the starters to complete the game. I received a warning letter from the league, escaping a fine.

My roommate, second baseman Tony Asaro, was from San Diego, California. He always bragged about San Diego's weather and complained about the *nasty weather* in New Jersey. It was true. In fact, he played in a winter league twice a week in San Diego. In spring training, I told him I would catch up to him in a week or two, which I did! We had good *chemistry* and made lots of double plays.

I was well on my way to having an outstanding season, when I suffered a severe groin injury. At the time of the injury (late June), I was hitting .320, leading the league in home runs with fifteen and leading the league in stolen bases. Confined to crutches, I missed the entire month of July. I came back, heavily taped, and hit one more home run. While not a power hitter, I was a pull hitter and our short (300 feet) right field fence, with a high screen, was in my favor. After the injury, if I hit one off the fence, I could get only a single. The Yankees knew about my injury, and they promoted me the following season to AA New Orleans of the Southern Association. I was voted Rookie of the Year in the Three-I League.

Peoria – 1957

BOTTOM OF THE THIRD:
New Orleans/
Professional Double
Play Record

New Orleans was a great city. We traveled by train (the last such travel in the minors). We had sleeper cars and occasionally, a few of us would sit outside on the caboose and watch the tracks disappear through the southern towns of Nashville, Memphis, and Chattanooga, Tennessee; Atlanta, Georgia; Mobile and Birmingham, Alabama; and Little Rock, Arkansas. Travel by train was great. We had our own car, next to the caboose. We had upper and lower berths, with the lower berth the better choice. On one trip, I jumped into the lower berth of an older player and closed the curtain. He opened the curtain and ousted me, saying he "could not make the climb." I gave way to seniority. We could also set up tables for card games and such.

I had an apartment on Canal Street and frequently visited Bourbon Street restaurants. A highlight from the New Orleans season: Our team set an organized baseball (major and minor league) double play record. We had 238 double plays, a record that, to my knowledge through research, still stands! Tony Asaro, our second baseman, was also promoted to New Orleans. The chemistry we had established the previous year at Peoria paid big dividends.

The Southern League was very competitive. In AA and AAA, there were young prospects as well as seasoned veterans, some ex-big leaguers. Some of my teammates eventually made it to the majors: Jack Reed, Ken Hunt, Tom Tresh, Russ Snyder, and Frank Leja, to name a few. Our manager was Charley Silvera, a former back-up catcher for Yogi Berra of the Yankees.

Our ballpark was a converted football stadium. Left field was real short with a high screen. A ball hit over the screen down the left field foul line to left center would be only a ground rule double. Right field was normal, 330 feet. Right-handed hitters had a distinct advantage.

It rained nearly every day in New Orleans. Baseball can be a grind. Few people realize that in the minor leagues, games take place six nights a week and Sunday afternoon. We used to "pray for rain" to have an occasional off night! We had an unprecedented stretch of seven consecutive game cancellations, due to heavy rain. We had to be at the baseball park around 4:30 p.m. each day. The rain would start around 3:00 p.m. and stop around 4:00 p.m. Minor league parks didn't have the luxury of tarp protection. We would call the park office at 4:00 p.m. and learn of the cancellation. We were happy our prayers had been answered! Makeup games, in the form of double headers, and one triple header later, were well worth the nights off.

Baseball being a *grind* leaves me with great sympathy toward umpires. In the minor leagues, umpires and players often stayed at the same hotel. After games, we sometimes engaged in conversation outside the hotel before calling it a night. Despite occasional disputes in the *heat of battle*, most were regular guys trying to make it to the big leagues, as well as the players. The umpires had a more difficult schedule than the players. Unlike players, umpires were always on the road, having no *home base*. After a three- or four-game series, they traveled to the next city on the schedule and another hotel. No off days and no home base made for a long season.

Speaking of umpires reminds me of a game later in my career and a difference of opinion with an umpire. In addition to their being a lonely group, umpires have a set of *unwritten rules*. They have a paranoid sense of being "shown up." Most fans aren't aware of the banter going on at home plate between the hitter and umpire and sometimes the pitcher. If an umpire called a strike on an obvious pitch out of the strike zone, the hitter might say, "That ball was low or very outside." In doing so, he had better not turn around and say it. This would be considered "showing up" the umpire in front of the fans, resulting in booing. I recall one tough umpire responding to my complaint by telling me to shut up and get in there and hit.

This brings me to the classic that I referred to earlier. The opposing pitcher had a very good sinker. It would get near the plate and sink, enticing me to swing. I would take the pitch and hear the umpire say, "Strike!" I would say, "That pitch was too low." This happened the first two times at bat. The ballpark had an electronic scoreboard in left field, with balls and strikes included. In a minor league park, the press box was close to home plate. Well, the third time at bat, I waited until the pitcher got his signal from the catcher, and I called time out. I turned to the press box and pointed to the scoreboard and told the scoreboard controller, "Put two strikes up on the board." The umpire (probably in shock) immediately said, "You're *outta* here!" He threw me out of the game. I suppose I won the battle and lost the war.

I played well enough to earn another promotion to AAA.

—New Orleans States Photos.

HUNT, right field; JACK REED, center field, and RUSS SNYDER, left field. The infielders are BILL DAVIDSON, shortstop; Tony Asaro, third base; Bob Maness, second base, and FRANK LEJA, first base.

ALL SET for their home debut is this 1958 edition of the Pelicans who'll do battle with Mobile tonight in City Park stadium. The outfielders packing their Louisville sluggers are, from left, RICHIE WINDLE, reserve outfielder; KEN

Pels Close Out Season Dropping Two to Chicks

Eleven Homers Blasted in Twin Bill

By BILL KEEFE

One more one-run reverse was added to the Pelicans astonishing record of "nose" defeats Sunday evening when the Memphis Chicks took both ends of the season's final doubleheader by 5 to 4 and 7 to 5.

Pushing all known records for home runs in one park was the total of 11 circuit clouts for the twin bill.

The biggest consolation the attendance of 240 paid enjoyed was the amazing completion of two double plays in the first game to give the Birds an all-

Pitcher Frank Baumann smacked a homer over the left field fence in the fourth to give the Chicks a 6 to 2 stranglehold on the contest, but in their half of the fourth the Pels took advantage of Baumann's wildness and, but for a brilliant catch by McCarthy of a terrific drive that Tresh would have put over the centerfield fence, the Pels most probably would have piled up more runs. Bill Davidson poled a long homer over the deep centerfield fence with two on — Hunt and Leja had walked — Baumann got out of the hole and was leading 6 to 5 as the fifth inning opened. Tony Asaro had homered in the first inning after Jack Reed had singled and that accounted for the Pels' first two runs.

In the opener Cereghino had the Chicks 4 to 3 after six innings and though the top half of the sixth was rocky for him, inasmuch as the Visitors loaded the bases with two down, but the big Pel pitcher came up with a grounder by McKee and retired the side.

Meanwhile Stablefeld had closed the gate on the Pels and turn defeat into victory for the Tribe.

time record of 238 for the season—16 more than a long-standing mark turned in by the Nashville Vols in 1952.

FIRST GAME

Memphis—	AB	R	H	RBI
Tanner 3b	3	1	1	0
Frazier 2b	4	1	1	0
McCarthy cf	4	0	0	0
Dipippo 1b	4	0	2	1
Sczesny rf	3	1	1	0
Comolli c	2	0	1	2
Grote lf	2	1	1	1
McKee ss	3	1	1	1
Stablefeld p	2	0	1	0
a-Rivich	1	0	0	0
Slack p	0	0	0	0
Totals	29	5	10	5

NEW ORLEANS—	AB	R	H	RBI
Reed cf	3	0	0	0
Asaro 2b	3	1	2	2
Hunt rf	2	1	1	2
Leja 1b	3	1	2	1
Snyder lf	4	0	0	0
Tresh 3b	4	1	1	0
Davidson ss	3	0	2	2
North c	2	0	0	0
Utley p	0	0	0	0
Cereghino p	3	0	0	0
Totals	27	4	8	4

a—Grounded out for Stablefeld in 7th.

Davidson, Asaro and Leja; Asaro, Davidson and Leja. LOB-Memphis 7, New Orleans 7. 2B-Davidson. Asaro Tresh, Dipippo. HR-Hunt, Comolli, McKee, Leja, Tanner. SB-Davidson. Tresh.

	IP	H	R	ER	BB	SO
Stbfld (W 8-10)	6	8	4	4	1	5
Slack	1	0	0	0	2	2
Crghn (L 9-16)	6⅔	10	5	5	0	0
Utley	⅓	0	0	0	0	0

WP-Cereghino, Stablefeld. U- Daugherty and Burns. T-1:45.

SECOND GAME

MEMPHIS—	AB	R	H	RBI
Tanner 3b	3	1	1	2
Frazier 2b	2	0	2	1
McCarthy cf	4	0	0	0
Dipippo 1b	2	2	2	0
Sczesny rf	2	2	2	1
Grote lf	3	0	0	2
Rivich c	3	0	0	0
Baumann p	2	2	2	1
Totals	25	7	10	7

NEW ORLEANS—	AB	R	H	RBI
Reed, cf	3	1	1	0
Asaro 2b	2	1	1	0
Hunt, rf	2	1	0	0
Leja 1b	1	1	0	0
Snyder, lf	2	0	0	1
Tresh, 3b	2	0	0	1
Davidson, ss	2	0	0	0
Maley, c	0	0	0	0
Utley p	0	0	0	0
a-Nardella	1	0	0	0
Henriksen, p	0	0	0	0
b-North	1	0	0	0
Yochim, p	0	0	0	0
Totals	21	5	3	5

a—Struck out for Utley in 3rd; b—Grounded out for Hendriksen in 4th. (Called end 6th because of curfew.)

Score by innings:
Memphis ..... 041 101—7
NEW ORLEANS ..... 200 300—5

Summary: E-Maley. McKee. PO-A-Memphis 18-5, New Orleans 18-11. LOB-Memphis 6, New Orleans 2. 2B-McCarthey, Frazier. HR-Asaro, Grote, Tanner, Sczesny, Baumann, Davidson. SB-Reed. S-Frazier. SF-Tresh.

TOP OF THE FOURTH:
Spring Training/Train to Richmond, Virginia/ Next Assignment

The Yankees had two AAA teams: Denver, Colorado, and Richmond, Virginia, when I signed a contract. Now, they were down to one—Richmond, Virginia, which was my assignment. Climbing the Yankees baseball ladder to AAA presented a problem because the Yankees were stocked with good players at that level. There were no openings on the Richmond roster for players like me and about twenty others. These players were considered top prospects in the Yankee organization. Many went on to the major leagues. Russ Snyder, who I played with in New Orleans, received a trade to the Kansas City organization and went on to a long career in the majors.

We broke camp in spring training and headed north on a train to Richmond, Virginia. We (Richmond) were in one car and the big club (Yankees) in another. An annual game between Richmond and the Yankees took place, after a parade, followed by dinner. The annual game always attracted capacity crowds. They roped off the outfield near the fences to control the crowd size. A chance to see Mickey Mantle and other star players perform accounted for the huge crowd.

Manager Casey Stengel of course was the featured speaker at the dinner. Casey, famous for his verbal blunders, made the dinner a memorable experience. All the Yankee players and coaches attended. They would head for New York the next day to prepare for the coming season.

I can remember the next day, watching the workout of the Richmond players who had made the team. Meanwhile, several of us were waiting for an assignment. We all had had good seasons the previous year and looked forward to a promotion. I suppose at this point, the enormity of my "dream" hit home. We all had the same dream, but achieving it wouldn't be easy.

BOTTOM OF THE FOURTH:
Miami/Pepper Martin

While waiting with the other players for an assignment, the Yankees summoned me to the office. They informed me that Miami (AAA International League) needed a shortstop right away. I arrived in Miami and found that their veteran shortstop, Foster Castleman, had a slight leg injury, wasn't covering much ground but was hitting over .400. I waited for my opportunity. My career was on hold. Although I wasn't playing, my short stint in Miami was an unforgettable experience. John "Pepper" Martin was the manager. Apart from New York Yankees' manager Casey Stengel, Pepper was the most unforgettable person I encountered in my eleven-year career. Pepper was the gregarious, life-of- the- party leader. I'll speak to some of his "antics" as they occurred.

Since I wasn't playing, I took advantage of the beautiful Miami beaches. I didn't, however, respect the Florida sun rays. I tried to hide the sunburn at the ballpark. I took quick showers; however, Pepper spotted me one night. "Billy, you're pink!" he exclaimed. Any other manager would probably have fined me.

All the players loved Pepper. In professional baseball, managers traditionally hold a clubhouse meeting on the first night of a new series. They do this to review the opposing team's hitters and pitchers, and so on, and to devise a game plan. Well, Pepper held a meeting EVERY night. He had this big, high-backed chair, and with his pipe in hand, he "held court." We had a mixture of young and veteran players. Though the meetings were serious, there were times he had all of us laughing. He was an amazing self-taught person. He had this penchant for learning and enjoying life. In meetings, he tried to use big words and phrases to describe events.

Pepper also coached third base. One game, our third baseman, Woody Smith, tried to score from second base on a single, despite Pepper's effort to hold him at third base. He was safe. The next night, Pepper had his usual pre-game meeting. He said "Woody, I tried to hold you up last night, but you came around third base with reckless abandon, and you were safe. I was the first one to congratulate you. I admire your adventurous spirit." All of us had a good laugh!

One of our pitchers was former major leaguer, Mickey McDermott. He was a nightclub singer in the off-season and good friends with Frank Sinatra. Mickey played for the Boston Red Sox. The Boston writers always had a reputation for being tough on players, even Ted Williams. After one tough outing, the writers described him as "juvenile delinquent Mickey McDermott." I roomed with Mickey in Havana, Cuba, and he told me Dom DiMaggio offered to buy him a suit if he would punch that writer in the mouth. It never happened!

Pepper had a routine of letting the next night's pitcher get his workout, shower, and sit in the stands for the game. Well, the next night, Pepper had his usual meeting and pointed out something that had happened in the game. Pepper asked, "Did you see that, Mick?" Mickey said, "Hell no, Pep! I was in a nightclub." Any other manager

I ever had would have exploded. Not Pepper. He laughed and simply went on to another play.

One night, we had a tough loss. As Pepper approached the dugout, a fan audibly questioned Pepper's judgment. Pepper stopped on the dugout step and began patiently explaining his strategy to the fan. His patience was incredible.

On another occasion, when I had dinner with Pepper, I noticed many interesting paintings hanging on the dining room wall. While we waited for our meal, Pepper offered thought-provoking comments on several of the paintings. His appreciation of and search for knowledge further demonstrated Pepper's enjoyment of life. He truly was "one of a kind."

We finished a two-week home stand, and I played sparingly. We left for a road trip to Montreal and Toronto, Canada, followed by visits to Richmond, Virginia, and Havana, Cuba. I enjoyed Montreal and Toronto. It was April and very cold, with fans wearing overcoats. I looked forward to warmer climates in Richmond and Havana.

Pepper Martin

Outfielder / Third baseman

TOP OF THE FIFTH:
Havana, Cuba/
Fidel Castro

Havana was quite an experience. Fidel Castro had ousted Cuban dictator Fulgencio Batista on January 1, 1959. It was now April 1959, and Fidel Castro was en route home after a meeting with the Council on Foreign Relations in New York City. Fidel's flight was scheduled to arrive about an hour after ours. Security at customs was very tight, filled with military personnel. It's about ten miles from the airport to downtown Havana. People lined the streets to welcome him on his return. Busloads of people were coming to the airport as we headed in the opposite direction to the Havana Hilton, our downtown hotel.

I got the impression that the Cuban people were genuinely happy, as reflected in their raucous shouts and cheers. Was it genuine? Or would it be more like a *ray of hope*, Castro vs. Batista?

The Hilton Hotel personnel were very friendly and didn't appear to be under stress. No unusual movements in the lobby. No signs of tension at the ballpark, including the Havana players. So, I was surprised to learn later, from my former teammates, that some turbulent times, perhaps due to the political climate and Cuban Revolution, were occurring.

I suppose the short four-day visit to Havana, on a tight schedule, restricted any extensive sightseeing. My walks downtown, with blocks of obvious poverty, and along the beautiful waterfront, gave no indication of tension. This proved to be my only visit to Havana. The Yankees sent me to Denver upon my return to Miami, which I will explain shortly.

Havana had a good baseball team. The Havana Sugar Kings were a Cuban-based minor league team, affiliated with the Cincinnati Reds. It was the International League, Class AAA. The Sugar Kings played in El Gran Estadio del Cerro (Gran Stadium). They finished third in the standings but upset Columbus and Richmond in the playoffs to win the league championship. They ended up winning the 1959 Junior World Series in seven games over the Minneapolis Millers of the American Association. Teams in the league included: Havana, Cuba; Buffalo and Rochester, New York; Columbus, Ohio; Miami, Florida; Richmond, Virginia; and Montreal and Toronto, Canada.

I remember one character on the Sugar Kings team: Lou Skizas. Casey Stengel called him one of the most natural right-handed hitters he ever saw. Lou had some nervous mannerisms when getting ready to hit. Before stepping into the batter's box, he would do several things—tug on his hat, rub his shirt, touch his nose, tap his bat on the ground, etc. He would continue this ritual while the pitcher was winding up to pitch. The last thing he did was touch a rabbit's foot in his back pocket for luck. *Surprisingly*, Lou acquired the nickname Nervous Greek. Players on the bench would wager on whether he would get his hands back on the bat in time to hit. He did and generally hit a line drive somewhere. Stengel was right!

It was common knowledge that Fidel loved baseball. One night after our game, manager Pepper Martin told some of us that Fidel was in the hotel dining room. All of us knew that Pepper loved to talk, and before long, he and Fidel were engaged in spirited baseball conversation. Fidel was in military fatigues, with ten or more of his soldiers, sitting at a long table.

Pepper began by telling stories about the "Gashouse Gang" of the old St. Louis Cardinals. Some of his teammates, such as Leo Durocher, Joe Medwick, and Dizzy Dean, received this designation due to their antics on and off the field. Enos Slaughter, for whom I later played in Houston, was also a member. In addition, Pepper bore the label "Wild Horse of the Osage," due to his daring, aggressive base running.

Fidel, an avid baseball fan, undoubtedly knew about Pepper's nickname and career. He obviously enjoyed the conversation, as laughter erupted. Then Pepper introduced me to Fidel. As he shook my hand, he commented, "So young." I was twenty-two at the time.

After we left Havana, the next team to arrive was Rochester. The Rochester Red Wings coach, Frank Verdi, and shortstop Leo Cardenas were reportedly grazed by gunshots. The Havana Sugar Kings homestand came to an end. They did, however, finish the season. The next year, 1960, Castro nationalized all U.S.-owned enterprises in Cuba, and on July 8,1960, Baseball Commissioner Ford Frick, under pressure from the secretary of state, announced that the Sugar Kings would move to Jersey City, New Jersey.

Professional baseball has not returned to Havana. I also learned from my former teammates that, in subsequent trips to Havana, Pepper and Fidel cemented their relationship. They would talk baseball for hours. After this season, Pepper finally retired. I'm sure Fidel missed Pepper and ultimately professional baseball.

For readers interested in this important time in Havana's history, I recommend *Waiting for Snow in Havana – Confessions of a Cuban*

Boy by Carlos Eire. This autobiography, published in 2003, won the National Book Award for Nonfiction.

Fidel Castro – 1959 manager Gene Mauch – second from left

BOTTOM OF THE FIFTH:
Denver, Colorado/ Marines Paris Island

I wasn't playing with Miami, and the Yankees weren't going to let me languish on the bench. Following our trip to Havana and return to Miami, the Yankees assigned me to Denver, Colorado, of the American Association (AAA).

Denver was a great place to play. Stan Hack was our manager. Our ballpark was located a few miles from downtown Denver. In later years, the Denver Broncos football team used our ballpark, which previously bore the name Bear Stadium. Our owner, Bob Howsam, had been actively seeking a Major League Baseball franchise for Denver. He learned that Denver would need a larger ballpark, and in 1960, they added more seats, for a total of 34,000.

Facing heavy debt, with no baseball franchise, Howsam resorted to football by acquiring a franchise from the AFL, the American Football League. The AFL Broncos played in Mile High Stadium from 1960 to 1966. The Broncos were an unsuccessful team and, unfortunately, Howsam lost a lot of money in their initial season. One million dollars was a hefty sum in the 1960s. He sold his business, losing the Broncos, the Bears, and Bear Stadium. The AFL-NFL merger (American Football League – National Football League) included Denver, on the condition that the seating would be expanded. This would be the home of the Broncos until it became a parking lot for their new Sports Authority Field at Mile High in 2001.

Denver received their Major League Baseball franchise and played their first two seasons, 1993 and 1994, at Mile High Stadium until they moved to their new downtown stadium, Coors Field. Bob Howsam never realized his dream; however, he enjoyed an outstanding career as a Cincinnati Reds general manager.

I was young, and little did I know that one day, I would visit my son Benjamin in Denver. He teaches school and lives there with his wife Karen, daughter Kyla, and son Evan. Prior to his marriage, I visited Ben, who was contemplating living in Denver, and my other son Will, who lived there while he worked on his master's degree at the University of Colorado. I enjoyed visiting the old ballpark, Bear Stadium, which had been remodeled for the Broncos. It brought back fond memories.

The American Association was a good league with teams, such as Houston, Dallas, Minneapolis, St. Paul, Omaha, Louisville, and Indianapolis. Hall of Fame pitcher Bob Gibson played for Omaha. We had several veteran players, some with major league experience. My roommate was second baseman, Bobby Malkmus, a former major leaguer.

In later years, a humorous story involving Bobby and myself occurred. When I attended a Hall of Fame dinner, one of my minor league general managers, who had become a Major League Baseball scout (talent recruiter), was present. Prior to dinner, the GM informed me that someone I knew was at his table. He walked me over and introduced me, but Bobby didn't recall our connection. I found it incredible that my roommate and double play partner couldn't remember me. I obviously made a great impression!

Of all the teams I played for in my eleven-year career, none matched this cast of characters. Clubhouse pranks occurred daily. I'll start with Bob Walz, a pitcher who always dressed in black—shoes, socks, pants, shirt, and sunglasses; even his hair was black! Bob loved horse racing and rushed from the race track to the ballpark to make the 4:30 p.m. reporting time. Gene Hassell, known as Little Man due to his short stature, always seemed to be in the middle of clubhouse happenings. Gene was friendly with a wealthy man in Denver, who was the same size, and Gene would accept some of his clothing and shoes. Florsheim shoes were among the best, and Gene would flaunt them. He would check other players' clothing and shoes. Walz would razz Little Man about his hand-me-downs. Little Man's response was, "They're better than those Worthmores (an off-brand of Florsheim's) you're wearing!" Walz accused Little Man of checking all our belongings. This clubhouse banter occurred daily, before and after the game.

One plane trip stands out. A storm developed, and the rain and lightning came, and the plane shook. My roommate, Bobby Malkmus, was a very religious person. I often found him back in the room after a game, writing passages from the Bible. On this flight, we were seatmates during the storm. Everyone was quiet and frightened. Little Man stood up in the front of the plane and said, "Woe be unto you sinners." Malkmus solemnly said, "Too late now, Little Man." Malkmus had a large nose, and Little Man put his fist and elbow up to Malkmus's nose and mocked him, "Too late now, Little Man."

Bob Oldis, an outstanding catcher, was also an interesting character. He was a showman. On a foul ball behind home plate, he would flip his mask off, go into a deep crouch, and pound his glove from the time it was hit until he caught it! Fans loved it.

On one road trip to Louisville, Kentucky, the marquee sign on the stadium read "The Denver Bears and the colorful Bob Oldis vs.

the Louisville Cardinals." In one game, he hit a single. He took a lead, and to everyone's amazement, had the first base bag behind his back! Umpires were aware of his antics and gave him a little leeway.

Gene Mauch got the Philadelphia Phillies manager's job over the winter. He selected Oldis and Malkmus from our team. Another player, Gordon Windhorn, received a bid from the Los Angeles Dodgers.

Tony Bartirome was a slick-fielding first baseman. He was only about 5 feet, 7 inches, short for a first baseman, but he played in the majors. He later became a trainer for the Pittsburgh Pirates. I always wondered how he qualified to be a trainer.

During the season, we often performed a pre-game phantom infield practice routine. Our coach would hit an imaginary ball to the infielders, and we would go through the motions of fielding and throwing the ball around the infield. We even mimicked double plays. It was very realistic, and fans applauded the performance.

All these players and incidents throughout the season made this the most unforgettable team in my career.

A hotel in downtown Denver featured a great piano bar. After a tough night at the ball yard, it was a good place to unwind and relax. David Whitfield, a British singer, had a 1954 hit, "Cara Mia." Well, there was a regular patron who sounded exactly like Whitfield. When he sang "Cara Mia," everyone within hearing distance directed their attention to the piano bar. It was spectacular! No talking, no singing, just enjoying the performance. The piano bar provided a relaxing atmosphere for me. It was a bonus if my "favorite singer" was in attendance. He never disappointed his followers.

After the Denver season, I had to focus on the military draft situation. It was 1959, and people of my age faced being drafted into the army for two years. From 1940 to 1973, men ages 18-25 received the draft call. This was necessary during the Vietnam War. Jerry Coleman, a former Yankee player, was the Yankees' minor league infield instructor. He was a major in the Marines, and he told me he could get me into the Marine Corps Reserve Program. This would allow me to finish six months of basic training and still be ready for spring training. It was a six-year obligation with two weeks of reserve training every year. Without hesitation, I joined and avoided losing two years of my career.

Due to my military obligation, I had to turn down an opportunity to play winter ball in Caracas, Venezuela. This may or may not have helped my career. Many players advanced their careers by playing winter league ball. Most of the leagues featured major league and AAA players, and the competition improved your skills. Some of the popular Latin American countries were Venezuela, Dominican Republic, Puerto Rico, Cuba, and Mexico. These countries received permission to bring a few players from the United States to fill their rosters. Competition was stiff. Most baseball fans think winter ball is a picnic, a vacation. WRONG! If a player got off to a slow start, he could be released and catching the next plane home. So, not all winter ball experiences are successful. I'll never know how I would have benefited.

My assignment was Paris Island, South Carolina, and while I remain proud to be a Marine, there were many nights I silently cursed Jerry Coleman. Paris Island's reputation is for real!

Art Rooney, the president of the Pittsburgh Steelers (NFL), was in our platoon. He received no favoritism from the drill instructors, who knew Art was the son of Art Rooney, Sr.

The Marines kindly accepted my appeal to satisfy my education at Temple University. They arranged for me to report to the Marine Headquarters in South Philadelphia for clerical duties. I reported in Marine dress uniform every day from 9:00 to 5:00. This allowed me to attend evening classes at Temple. Otherwise, I would miss an entire semester. I already missed the second of two semesters due to my baseball career. I was very grateful for this opportunity to obtain my college degree.

I almost forgot to mention a ritual that I followed upon joining a new team. When I needed transportation, I always purchased an old car for $100.00 and sold it for $200.00. When I left Miami for Denver, I sold my car to Mickey McDermott. He sent me a letter in Denver, cursing me out, for the car breaking down in the middle of

Biscayne Blvd. I had neglected to tell him that he needed to add water every day. I apologized. When the Denver season ended, I broke tradition and drove my junk car from Denver to New Jersey.

Denver 1959

Davidson seated second from right

Denver Bear Stadium – 1959

TOP OF THE SIXTH:
Houston/Enos Slaughter

It took me two days to drive across the country from Denver to New Jersey, stopping at bowling alley parking lots to catch some ZZZs. Only once did I stop at a motel because I was too tired to sleep along the road, which I deemed too risky.

I made it home safely in my junk automobile. I left a few weeks later for Paris Island. Marines basic training was tough, however I made it through and got out in time for spring training, as planned. I had only a brief time with family and friends before leaving for Florida to begin spring training. The year was 1960, and the competitive AAA level with the Yankees remained.

With the major leagues in those days having only eight teams in each league, a logjam at the AA and AAA level was a reality. Every now and then, a close friend, Ron Rossi, and I reflect on this very subject. We both signed with top organizations. Ron was a great athlete who signed with the Dodgers, and I with the Yankees. Although Ron didn't play as long as I did, we agree that these two organizations were at the top on fundamentals and the most difficult to advance to the major leagues.

With the Yankees *loaded* at the AAA level, I once again waited for an assignment. They sent me to Amarillo in the Texas League for a few weeks and finally assigned me to Houston in the American Association (AAA). Once again, players from another organization surrounded me. This never bothered me, however, since my new teammates respected the Yankee organization. Make no mistake, though, I *felt* like I had to prove myself to the new group. Houston was a Chicago Cubs organization. Ninety percent of the players started with the Cubs organization, working their way up the ladder, hopefully to the major leagues.

We had a good ball club, managed by Hall of Fame player Enos Slaughter. As I mentioned previously, Enos and Pepper Martin were members of the St. Louis Cardinals "Gas House Gang." Occasionally, Enos would play in the outfield if we were short on players, due to injury. He could still hit! Enos had a few idiosyncrasies, and I remember teasing him on occasion. He chewed tobacco on the bench and invariably insisted on sitting in the same spot in the dugout every game. I waited my chance and occupied his seat, only to be chased. We had our own plane (DC-3), and, you guessed it, Enos had to sit in the same seat there too. He chased me again, all in good fun.

One amusing story involving Enos took place in Dallas, Texas. In professional baseball, each player receives a few complimentary game tickets for family and friends. Our pitcher, Al Lary, asked me if he could use my tickets if I didn't need them. He was from Dallas, and I had no need for the tickets. Typically, after a game, we have a bite to eat and unwind with a beverage or two of our choice.

Well, our general manager made the short trip from Houston and saw his "girlfriend" on the will call list. Trouble was, it was under my name. I was innocent! I guess I was a little late getting back to my room.

Our coach told me the next day that our GM and Enos were in the lobby, and he ordered Enos to call my room. My roommate, Dick Bertell, answered. Enos asked, "Is Davidson there?" Dick said I was sleeping. Enos said "Wake him up." Dick knew I wasn't there. He came back and said, "He just stepped out for a cup of coffee." Enos said, "Coffee's ass" and hung up.

Enos said at a meeting the next night, "A few of you guys were out last night. You'll know who you are by the size of your check." Luckily, we never did get fined.

We had two future Hall of Fame players on our club—third baseman Ron Santo and outfielder Billy Williams. Opposing players would stop what they were doing to watch Billy in batting practice. Apart from Ted Williams (Boston Red Sox), Billy was the best left-handed hitter I've ever seen. Ron became a top broadcaster for Chicago Cubs games.

Roger Hornsby, a Hall of Fame member, was a hitting instructor for the Chicago Cubs organization. Once he was in Houston for a home series. I took advantage of this and came out early for extra hitting practice under his watchful eye. Throughout my career, I felt plagued by "pulling" the ball too much. Ironically, this was a strength in high school and amateur leagues. Some players had difficulty pulling the ball. However, in professional baseball, it is a weakness. The more you "spray" the ball to all fields, the better. Pitchers take advantage of any weakness. I knew this and worked on correcting it. However, perfecting something is difficult in AA and AAA ball. In batting practice, I could hit to all fields with ease, but in the game, I would resort to pulling the ball. Roger watched me one day and told me not to change a thing. In high school and later, I had had good coaches, and my father was knowledgeable, but no one *stressed* the importance of spraying the ball. A strength became a weakness and haunted me throughout my career. Young players should TAKE HEED.

It was a lot of fun playing against Denver and my former teammates. One memorable experience was a flight to Denver from Houston. Our pilot decided to refuel in Omaha, Nebraska, and he inadvertently landed at a Strategic Air Command (SAC) airfield. We arrived unannounced because someone in the control tower had fallen asleep. As we got off the plane, we were surrounded by soldiers, rifles in hand. It was 3:00 a.m., and they ordered us to stand outside until an official cleared us. I often wonder what discipline the soldier in the control tower received.

YANKEES — When Billy Davidson signed with the New York Yankees (left) he got to sit in front of Ralph Houk, a future manager, in the 1957 rookie camp team picture. With Houston (above) in 1960, he played with future Hall of Famer Billy Williams (right).

BOTTOM OF THE SIXTH:
Nashville/Sulphur Dell

In the baseball off-season, I continued pursuing my degree. I worked as a substitute school teacher during the day and took classes at Temple University in the evening. I was close to my degree and working toward obtaining it, satisfying school district guidelines.

Spring arrived, and I was ready for Florida and baseball spring training. I was still *owned* by the Yankees, with a Richmond contract. The Yankees decided to let Richmond "test" Fort Lauderdale for a possible spring training site in the future. Fort Lauderdale was beautiful. The Yankees evidently thought likewise, as it became their new facility the following year. Richmond would be *banished* to less attractive pastures.

My assignment was Nashville, Tennessee, of the Southern Association (AA). Jerry Coleman, seeing how the Yankee organization had blocked me, advised me to ask for my release. They denied my request. This was prior to any Player Association Union. Teams owned their players. There were no options, they had complete control. I remember receiving a letter one off- season, regarding a AAA or minor league union. It never got off the ground. We had no choice in accepting their terms of salary or assignments. Little did I realize my Nashville assignment would be very instrumental in providing inspiration for my future book.

Nashville was one of my favorite cities. The Nashville "Vols" played in historic Sulphur Dell, which no longer exists. It was such a unique stadium.

The outfield featured steep hills, right field being the steepest. Right field also had the closest fence (262 feet), with a 30-foot screen on top of the fence. If a player hit a line drive to right field over the second baseman's head, he had to *run like hell* to first or the right fielder would throw him out at first base. Balls hit off the right field screen would carom over the right fielder's head, and the second baseman would have to retrieve it. On balls hit between the outfielders, they would have the difficult task of running on a side hill, at the same time keeping their eye on the ball. I remember one stretch when I got on base ten consecutive times—two home runs and eight walks. Sulphur Dell was built in 1869 and demolished in 1969.

Sulphur Dell – Nashville – 1961

TOP OF THE SEVENTH:
Nashville/
Grand Ole Opry

Once I arrived in Nashville, I decided to stay in a hotel until I found an apartment. One of my teammates, Rod Kanehl, had a good year with Nashville, and the following year, the New York Mets chose him in their expansion draft. The Mets and the Houston Astros were new major league expansion teams. Rod informed me that his wife was joining him, and I could have his apartment. He shared an apartment with a bartender, who was a Navy retiree. I accepted his offer, and Charley (his actual name) the bartender proved to be a great guy. It seemed like he knew everyone.

As I mentioned earlier, the Grand Ole Opry and historic Ryman Auditorium held a special fascination for me. Opry performers, including Patsy Cline, Jim Reeves, Marty Robbins, Minnie Pearl, and others, had seats at the Sulphur Dell ballpark, with their names on the back of the seats. As luck would have it, Charley knew the house bass player. He introduced me, and we became friends. Every Saturday night, he would let me in the side door, and I sat offstage in the wings. Technicians in a radio booth offstage, directly above my head, recorded the Saturday night performance. For the benefit of the radio audience, someone would raise placards with *APPLAUD* written on them after a performance. Marty Robbins and Patsy Cline didn't require a placard. I remember people in the audience fanning themselves, due to the absence of air conditioning.

On one occasion, after her performance, Patsy Cline said to those of us sitting in the wings, "Let's send out for a pizza." They were down-to-earth people who gave me a lasting respect for country music performers.

Mingling with these icons was an unforgettable experience. I looked forward to Saturday nights. I would hurry to the Opry after our game. After the performance, everyone went to Ernest Tubbs's record shop for a "jamboree."

Grand Ole Opry Stage

Grand Ole Opry

BOTTOM OF THE SEVENTH:
Austin/Mexico

Unexpectedly and disappointingly, my stay in Nashville was short lived. I was the shortstop for over a month, and, to my surprise, a Cincinnati organization player supplanted me. As I alluded to earlier, this often happens in professional baseball. However, my short stay in Nashville left lasting impressions.

I naturally balked at this development and again asked the Yankees for my release. I finally obtained it, and, although it wouldn't be easy, I was now on my own and free to make negotiations. I had made some connections during my career and had some phone numbers. I called several minor league directors in different organizations, inquiring about possible openings. Having asked for my own release and coming from a top organization, the Yankees, were factors in my favor. I was "unemployed" for only a short time. I was signed by the Milwaukee Braves organization and optioned to Austin of the Texas League.

Some highlights of my stay in Austin include a future Hall of Fame teammate, pitcher Phil Niekro; first baseman Tommy Aaron (Hall of Fame Hank Aaron's brother), and a two-week Pan American Series with the Mexican League. Niekro featured a knuckleball that reminded me of another Hall of Fame pitcher, Hoyt Wilhelm. The Pan American series was interesting. We played in Mexico cities for two weeks, and their teams visited Texas League teams for two weeks. All games counted in the standings for each league.

We played in Mexico City, Puebla, Poza Rica, and Veracruz. Except for Mexico City, poverty prevailed. Veracruz had families living in the outfield stands corridor. Laundry dried on clothes lines near ticket booths. We had to change at the hotel, as kids would steal our belongings in the clubhouse or dugout. Holding your glove tightly after the game was a given. Puebla featured a converted bullfighting arena for a ballpark.

As I'm writing, I find it incredible that many cities, including Austin, would have a connection in later life. Whenever I joined a new team, I inquired about lakes or pools in the area, where I could relax prior to night games. I was informed of an unusual pool, *Barton Springs*. It featured lawns and terraced steps on each side, the length of the pool. Spring water was let in at one end, pooling at the far end.

After my retirement, my wife and I visited my son, Will, who had accepted a job in Austin. I asked him about the pool. He said it was right behind his apartment, which he could view from his balcony, high above the pool, on a grassy knoll. Swimming in the pool brought back memories.

One of the teams in our league was San Antonio, Texas. We stayed at a downtown hotel. While I did some sightseeing near the hotel, I looked over a railing and gazed at an unusual sight. It was the famous *River Walk*, beneath the city streets. Canals, shops, and restaurants were featured, many with strolling mariachi bands. So, naturally, whenever we visited Will in Austin, we would take the

70-mile drive to San Antonio. The River Walk and the Alamo became destinations.

Austin was a great city. The Texas League was competitive, and I had a decent year. Teams in the league included Austin, Amarillo, San Antonio, and Victoria in Texas, and Ardmore and Tulsa in Oklahoma. The Milwaukee organization didn't own me. I had signed a one-year contract, and I was free to negotiate the following spring.

Barton Springs Pool Austin, Texas

River Walk San Antonio, Texas

River Walk San Antonio, Texas

Veracruz, Mexico

TOP OF THE EIGHTH:
Hawaii

I n the winter of 1961, I visited Lee McPhail in Baltimore, Maryland. Lee McPhail, of the iconic McPhail baseball family, was the general manager of the Baltimore Orioles. He was the one responsible for my signing with the New York Yankees. Lee was an easy-going, soft-spoken gentleman, and he listened to my vagabond career path to date. He knew I had given up a lot (basketball scholarship at Temple University) to sign with the Yankees. I knew I would have a sympathetic ear; everyone in baseball respected Lee. He made phone calls and connected me with Hawaii (California Angels organization). We had spring training in San Bernardino, California, and it was a pleasant change. All my previous springs were spent in Florida. I thanked Lee and looked forward to spring.

I made the team and headed for Hawaii. Irv Noren, a former Yankee, was the manager and made me feel welcome. ALOHA! Life was great, playing baseball in beautiful Hawaii.

Hall of Fame broadcaster, Harry Kalas, was the play-by-play announcer for Hawaii. He began his major league career with Houston, followed by a long career with the Philadelphia Phillies.

Baseball had expanded to Houston and the New York Mets. I remember a pitcher and I who played together in Nashville, sending a telegram to our former teammate Rod Kanehl. Rod was playing with the Mets, and we told him to "eat your heart out." That's how great it was playing in Hawaii. However, it wasn't the majors.

Staying in the Waikiki Biltmore Hotel until the season started was first class. We received a basket of fresh fruit, placed outside our room, each morning. There was a valley behind the hotel. Several times, we were treated to a beautiful view of a rainbow. Two of us leased an apartment when the season started. It was about a block from Waikiki Beach, which we visited daily. Every time I see a movie or a travel ad featuring Waikiki Beach, I think of walking gingerly through the coral, with Diamond Head volcano, an Oahu landmark, in clear view.

We didn't have to be at the ballpark until 4:00 p.m. Once again, life was great. However, I found myself playing a reserve role, which I reluctantly had accepted. California Angel players were favored, as they were good players who grew up in their farm system. Nick Morgan, the owner of the Hawaii franchise, had a connection with Japan and offered me a position. Since I was young, only twenty-four years old, I felt I still had opportunities in the states. Most players went to Japan near the end of their career. I declined.

Lee McPhail hadn't made any promises; he just offered me an opportunity. For that, I was thankful. An opening developed in the Chicago White Sox organization with Savannah, Georgia. They offered me a contract, and I accepted. Aloha!

BOTTOM OF THE EIGHTH:
Savannah/Pete Rose

Savannah became one of my favorite cities. In later years, my wife and I visited Savannah frequently. I had an apartment near downtown, across the street from the historic De Soto Hotel. One night, there was a disturbance at the De Soto. It was reported that Robert Mitchum, the movie star, was angry over poor room service. Mitchum was in town for the filming of *Cape Fear*.

Savannah is famous for its streets, consisting of squares, featuring parks inside the squares. It is a unique concept that highlights the historic homes with their ornate designs. It also has a built-in benefit of eliminating speeding on side streets.

A famous movie and book, *Midnight in the Garden of Good and Evil*, takes place in Savannah. The Mercer House, located in one of the squares, plays a major role in this true story. Actors John Cusack and Kevin Spacey play leading roles. Currently, it is named the

Mercer-Williams House. Johnny Mercer was a famous songwriter, and Jim Williams was an antique dealer and a historic home renovator. Williams purchased the house from the Mercer family.

Forrest Gump, with actor Tom Hanks, was another film that used Savannah as a backdrop. Forrest was seen sitting on a park bench in one of the squares.

One major street, Victory Drive, provided an enjoyable drive from my apartment to the ballpark. This scenic route featured live oak trees on which hung Spanish moss. It provided a spectacular visual effect with the moss-covered branches connecting over the street in a canopy effect. The scenic, five-mile drive also features historic southern homes, each one more spectacular than the other.

Bonaventure Cemetery is a tourist destination. Located near the Wilmington River, it features incredible statues and monuments, dating from the late 1800s. Johnny Mercer's grave is here, with select titles of his numerous songs engraved on marble benches and gravestones. An adjacent cemetery plays a central theme in the aforementioned movie, *Midnight in the Garden of Good and Evil.*

One night, after a game, a teammate suggested going to dinner at a restaurant named Boar's Head along the river. The restaurant, on the second floor, is in an old section of former cotton warehouses. This six-block area evolved into what now is a thriving tourist attraction along the river. Restaurants, shops, and riverboat cruises now occupy the site, with the historic warehouse look, a major attraction.

Whenever my wife and I visit Savannah, a drink at the Boar's Head, with a picture window providing a view of the river, is a must. The Boar's Head sign at the entrance, says, "Established in 1964." I enjoy telling the bartender or owner, "I had a drink here in 1962." The surprised owner informed me I was right; the original owner purchased it in 1959 and sold it. On a recent trip, I noticed a new awning at the entrance with the correct date.

It's easy to visualize how playing baseball for a living in such a beautiful and historic city made for an enjoyable experience. Of course, my wife and I visited the ballpark, and, while it has been remodeled, it still "looks the same."

Savannah was a Chicago White Sox affiliation. It was here that I first encountered the racial discrimination of the 1960s while playing baseball. The African American fans had to stay in a bleacher section in the outfield, along the left field foul line, not connected with the regular grandstand. Being from the North, I found this lack of acceptance to be a new experience. Two of our star players, Deacon Jones and Don Buford, were African Americans. During one game, Deacon looked for his wife in the outfield bleachers and couldn't locate her. There was a commotion in the grandstand behind home plate. The wives of Deacon and Don had taken seats in the *whites only* section and wouldn't leave, despite our General Manager Tom Flemings's pleas. The next night, they returned, saying it was too hot in the bleachers. Looking back, this incident preceded the Rosa Park incident and became one of many historic racial experiences I personally witnessed during my baseball career.

In July, the NAACP boycotted the stadium. Attendance had dwindled. Owner Bill Ackerman considered relocating. Lynchburg, Virginia, was actively looking for a team for the following year; however, they offered to accommodate the team for the remainder of the season. It was the end of July and in an *unprecedented* decision, Mr. Ackerman severed the Savannah connection and moved to Lynchburg for the last month of the season.

Another team in our league, Macon, Georgia, was rough on our African American players. I recall games being halted due to firecrackers thrown onto the field near our players. Minor league ballparks, being smaller than the major leagues', brought the fans closer to the playing field. Shouts of racial slurs were common, and the proximity magnified the tensions.

Off we went to a Lynchburg hotel where we lodged for the remainder of the season. Lynchburg was a nice city (very hilly) with a good ballpark. Savannah was gone but not forgotten.

The teams in the league included Macon and Augusta, Georgia; Greenville, South Carolina; Asheville and Charlotte, North Carolina;

Knoxville, Tennessee; and Portsmouth, Virginia. We had a good team—future big leaguers Don Buford, Deacon Jones, J.C. Martin, Dennis Higgins, Fred Talbot, Manly "Shot" Johnston, and future National Basketball Association Hall of Fame player Dave DeBusschere, to name a few. We were the regular season champions, with a 92-47 record; however, we lost to Macon in the playoffs 0-3.

Manly "Shot" Johnston, a 6-foot 3-inch, 235-pound pitcher, won twenty games. He was also a good power hitter and played outfield when not pitching. Shot gave me the ultimate compliment after clinching our pennant, calling me one of the best competitors he ever had played with. It was nice, coming from such a *warrior*.

Dave DeBusschere went 10-1, with a 2.49 earned run average. Dave knew I had played basketball at Temple. I told him the best backcourt combo in college history was Guy Rodgers and Hal Lear. He wasn't fond of Rodgers, having played against him in the NBA.

I used to challenge Dave to a one-on-one game, on one condition: no backing in, using his height advantage (6 feet vs. 6 feet, 6 inches). The challenge never materialized, primarily due to the summer heat during the baseball season. Just as well, reflecting on his NBA career. In spring training, Dave told me the Chicago White Sox wanted him to give up basketball. Dave said no way. I'll probably give up baseball.

We had a good team and a lot of fun together. Les Moss was "all business" as a manager and created a game-within-a-game incentive. A fine system was established for game situations, with the money going toward a party at the end of the season. If a player failed to drive a runner home from third base, with less than one out: $5.00. Failing to advance a runner on second base to third, with zero outs: $5.00. Missing a steal or hit and run sign: $5.00. Aside from game situations, he established other fines. Late to the ballpark: $10.00. Late for a road trip departure: $10.00. A "kangaroo court," consisting of coaches and the manager, would *listen* to any fine challenges. I don't recall anyone winning a challenge.

Macon, Georgia, had a future major league great, Pete Rose, playing second base. My first impression of Pete Rose was "who is this guy, running to first base on a walk?" It didn't take long to discover that his *extreme* hustle matched his ability. He was a switch-hitting second baseman, who had this extraordinary knack of getting on base. As a shortstop, he was a challenge to defend, but I robbed him of a hit on occasion. Baseball players sometimes stayed in a hotel, in lieu of finding an apartment. I did it myself in Denver and saved money in the process. When going on a road trip, we checked our extra belongings in storage and checked back into the hotel upon our return. Apartments were the norm; however, this was an option. Pete stayed in the visiting player's hotel, and I discovered he was a great guy. He would spot me in the lobby and acknowledge a hit taken away from him, "Hey, Davey, what are you doing robbing me?"

Little did I know he would someday be the HIT KING, breaking Ty Cobbs's record with 4,256 base hits. I hope that soon he will be voted into the Hall of Fame. He would be the nineteenth major league player I played with or against to enter the Major League Baseball Hall of Fame. Good luck, Pete!

Since I retired, my wife and I enjoy visiting Las Vegas on occasion. Pete has a memorabilia concession in a shop located in the Mandalay Bay Hotel.

I found an old Savannah versus Macon baseball program in the attic, containing both rosters. Pete was in Macon, and both rosters contained future Major League Baseball stars. I said to my wife, "This program would be a great item for Pete to sign."

I wasn't sure whether Pete would be interested. However, knowing his reputation for retaining anything connected to baseball, I thought he might enjoy it. I was right. Pete was genuinely interested, scrutinizing the program and rosters. In fact, before he even opened the program, he remarked, "You guys pulled out of Savannah near the end of the season." What a memory! He was very gracious and signed a baseball, "To a real gamer."

Bill, Ellen, Pete Rose

Boars Head Restaurant Savannah, Georgia

Bonaventure Cemetery – exquisite statuary Savannah, Georgia

Mercer House

Steamboat Gothic, Antebellum architecture found along many Savannah streets

TOP OF THE NINTH:
"Davidson, You Bum!"

The following season, I found myself back in Lynchburg, Virginia. Having finished the 1962 season in Lynchburg and winning the regular season championship, we received great acceptance from the fans. This, despite losing to Pete Rose's Macon team in the playoffs.

Les Moss, an excellent manager, was back. Les was a former major league catcher and naturally was great with pitchers. A manager's handling of pitchers is very important in the minor leagues, as they don't have the luxury of a pitching coach that major league managers enjoy.

The Southern League (AA) was strong, consisting of teams in Macon, Georgia; Asheville and Charlotte, North Carolina; and Chattanooga, Knoxville, and Nashville, Tennessee.

The racial tensions of this period in the South were obvious. As mentioned previously, Macon was particularly rough on African American players. On road trips throughout the South, I recall our teammates bringing African American players a bite to eat on "pit" stops. Later in the season, we noticed one change on a road trip to Knoxville. What made this trip unusual? It was the first time that African American players could stay with their teammates in the hotel. Previously, we had dropped the players off in an African American community and continued to our hotel.

One city in our league, Charlotte, provided me with an amusing incident and long-lasting memories. I was selected by one fan as a focal point for his opposition "needling." His timing was perfect. It would be quiet after the announcement of the pending National Anthem, prior to the start of the game. "DAVIDSON, YOU BUM!" echoed throughout the stadium.

This practice is not unusual. The next time you attend a major league game, take notice of some fans who are *constantly* berating the opposition. They shout personal remarks and obscenities and sometimes target *home team* players. Gene Mauch, a brilliant baseball tactician, did not escape fan "abuse." Mauch, a former Boston Red Sox player, managed Minneapolis, Minnesota, a AAA team in the American Association. While playing with Denver, I recall hearing a fan verbally assault Mauch the entire game. The fan brought up incidents from Mauch's minor and major league career and personal insults. This would go on for the entire four-night series. I admired Mauch's restraint.

We went on to St. Paul for a series, and I recall reading an article stating a time when Mauch "snapped" and went into the stands after this fan during a game. I'm not sure of the outcome, however, I have *zero* empathy for that fan.

Unlike the Gene Mauch's fan confrontation, my experience was free of violence. I'll return to the fan in Charlotte. He selected other quiet moments for the same, "DAVIDSON, YOU BUM!" Of course, my teammates and I felt amused. The next day, I went downtown and visited a novelty shop. I purchased a glass, with a beer-and-foam look. That night at game time, I waited for the fan to holler, you guessed it, "DAVIDSON, YOU BUM!" I placed the glass on the dugout roof. I spotted the fan and yelled "Have another beer!" Our players and fans near our dugout laughed and enjoyed the exchange. It was a three-game series, with more amusement to come.

The next night, while kneeling in the on-deck circle, which was close to the stands, two elderly ladies asked me why the fan picks on me. He usually started on me in the on-deck circle and in the batter's box. This night, I put two long pieces of cotton in my ears and didn't remove them until I was in the batter's box. The catcher and the umpire and fans near home plate laughed. Funny thing, I got a base hit and mimicked Jackie Gleason, arms flapping, running to first base. The next day a sportswriter wrote, "Bill Davidson, shortstop of the Lynchburg White Sox, added a little levity to the all-too-serious business of baseball at Griffith Park last night. After the first base railbirds had ridden him unmercifully through the first eight innings, Davidson came out to the on-deck circle with cotton stuffed into his ears. He removed the cotton when he went to bat and singled in Lynchburg's final run in a 7-1 win." I saved the clipping. The writer omitted the one stand-out fan and DAVIDSON, YOU BUM!

After the Charlotte series, we continued our road trip to Asheville, North Carolina. The next night, we stood for the National Anthem, prior to the game. To my astonishment, "DAVIDSON, YOU BUM!" reverberated throughout the stadium. Incredibly, he *followed* me to Asheville! My son Will lives in Asheville with his fiancée, April Spencer, and on a few visits, he obtained tickets for a game. The ballpark is still the same and brings back memories. Standing for the National Anthem, I half expect to hear the fan from Charlotte.

We finished our road trip and headed home to Lynchburg, Virginia. The next night just prior to the National Anthem, the ramp leading to the stadium held "my friend" from Charlotte and his usual refrain, "DAVIDSON, YOU BUM!" UNBELIEVABLE!

On our next trip to Charlotte, someone introduced me to this fan, and I learned that he evidently had randomly selected me for the jeers. Hard to believe, however, the story will remain in my memory bank forever.

BOTTOM OF THE NINTH:
Lynchburg, Virginia
Birth of Son, Will

The following spring, 1964, I attended spring training with the Chicago White Sox AAA team, Indianapolis, Indiana. Once again, I found myself surrounded by strangers—coaches and players who had grown up in the Chicago organization. Competing for a spot on the Indianapolis roster was difficult. My assignment to Lynchburg, Virginia, was disappointing, but I reunited with a great manager, Les Moss, and other former teammates. I got along great with Les, and while he rooted for me to stay with Indianapolis, he seemed happy to have added strength in the middle infield. Players must make the most of situations and work toward having a good season. I learned from Rod Kanehl, my former teammate in

Nashville, that one great year can get you a promotion. Rod went from AA to the major leagues—and the New York Mets—after an outstanding season.

As usual, the Southern League was strong. The teams included Lynchburg, Virginia; Macon and Columbus, Georgia; Charlotte and Asheville, North Carolina; Birmingham, Alabama; and Knoxville and Chattanooga, Tennessee.

Birmingham had some outstanding players: Rick Monday, Sal Bando, Vida Blue, and John "Blue Moon" Odom, to name a few. Birmingham was a Kansas City farm team, and these players went on to have good careers in the major leagues.

Kansas City owner, Charlie Finley, had the reputation of a *maverick*. He was the person responsible for changing the color scheme of major league uniforms. He introduced green, white, and gold colors. Before this, the standard was white for home uniforms, and gray for the road. Kansas City would eventually move to Oakland, California, presently called the Oakland Athletics.

We had nine games left in the season and lagged three games behind Birmingham in the standings. Word leaked that Finley promised all the Birmingham players color TVs if they won the pennant. We went to Birmingham for a three-game series and won all three. Now we were in a tie. We continued our road trip to Asheville for a three-game series. We won all three. Birmingham won their remaining three games at home. We remained tied in the standings. Incredibly, the last three games of our season featured BIRMINGHAM at LYNCHBURG! We won the first two games and the league championship. The last game didn't matter. A spectacular finish to a great season!

I saved the best for last. It was August 14, 1964, a few weeks before the end of the season. I was at the hospital for the birth of my first child. It was a boy! I played a game that night and left for a one-week road trip. The saying, "the show must go on" applied in baseball. Chico Fernandez, our second baseman, and his wife stood in proxy for the christening. It was a good season. The highlight of the season—the birth of my son, Will.

Chico, Wife and Will Lynchburg, Virginia 1964

Lynchburg White Sox – 1964 Davidson seated third from right

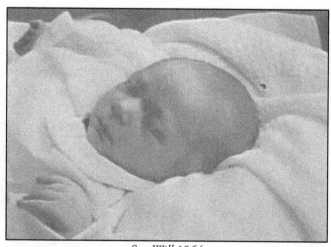

Son Will 1964

EXTRA INNINGS, TOP OF THE TENTH:

Indianapolis/Lynchburg/ Montgomery

My contract arrived in 1965, and my assignment was Indianapolis, Indiana. Spring training took place in Sarasota, Florida. Les Moss, my manager the past two seasons in Lynchburg, Virginia, received a promotion and was now the manager of Indianapolis. Don Bacon, a former teammate at Lynchburg, retired and now was a lower minor league manager in the Chicago White Sox organization. Don attended all the meetings and told me in confidence that Les lobbied for me to be on the Indianapolis roster. Despite two veteran ex-major league shortstops on the roster, I made the cut.

We broke camp and headed for Indianapolis. Two weeks went by, and I received little playing time. Les informed me that I had a new assignment: Lynchburg. I believe the White Sox hierarchy overruled Les, making my stay short-lived.

Off I went, back to Lynchburg. The season was already in progress, and a young prospect had the position of shortstop. Of course, I expressed my dissatisfaction and ultimately requested a solution. The Detroit Tigers organization arranged a trade. My new assignment was Montgomery, Alabama, and Lynchburg received a player in return. Both teams were in the same Southern League. Montgomery needed a shortstop and knew I was available. At least I felt wanted and chose to stay positive.

Playing against your former teammates is always a unique experience. While playing for Montgomery, I met George Wallace, the governor of Alabama, who became quite a controversial political figure. He was a big baseball fan and frequently attended games.

My roommate in Montgomery was pitcher Mike Marshall, a unique individual. Mike started his career in the Philadelphia Phillies organization as a shortstop. He had a strong arm and converted to pitching. It's an understatement to say that not many players shared a fondness for Mike. He was a stoic individual, very intelligent, with an aloof personality. I got along fine with Mike and found his antics amusing. A Michigan State University student (a few credits short of his degree) at a time when not many players attended college may have contributed to his attitude. Mike and I took advantage of perks, like being invited to private golf clubs. Although we got along, he always exhibited a sense of superiority. I remember saying, as we checked into our hotel room, "Room 204, the same exact room as last trip." Mike replied, "That's redundant."

In a game, Mike pitched, and I played shortstop. The batter hit a hard grounder between short and third for a hit. In the dugout, Mike said for everyone to hear, "You should have fielded that ball." I was livid. I said, "You have to be kidding! That ball was hit like a bullet." In professional ball, you *never* blame your teammates.

The players' wives generally sat behind home plate during ballgames. Look for little kids running around, and it's a good bet they belong to the players. Mike's wife, Nancy, would be in the stands, and when Mike pitched, she would yell "Come on, Mike, win it by yourself." This didn't endear her to the other wives. It seems like Montgomery was a precursor of things to come for the Marshalls.

Mike eventually pitched in the major leagues, winning the Cy Young Award for pitchers in 1974. Mike eventually earned three degrees, including a PhD in Kinesiology.

Controversy seemed to follow Mike. I remember reading about Mike being charged with trespassing at the Michigan State campus while attempting to gain access to a locked gate at an athletic field to work out.

Jim Bouton wrote a controversial book in 1970, titled *Ball Four*. Bouton and Mike were teammates on several teams. I find it very humorous that these two individuals with abrasive personalities would be the subjects of another controversial book in 1983 titled *Home Games*. The authors, Bobbie Bouton and Nancy Marshall, were the players' wives. Both players eventually divorced. Bobbie and Nancy maintained their friendship, and they reveal letters and journals in their book.

Racial tensions persisted during this period. African American teammates continued to receive racial slurs at the ballpark. I cringed at some of the remarks and admired the recipients' calm restraint. Perhaps if one receives such frequent verbal abuse, they find it easier to digest. I have often wondered why the Philadelphia Phillies assigned their prize prospect, Dick Allen, to Little Rock, Arkansas, in 1963; however, this was their only AAA team. Perhaps it was their only option.

Montgomery was very hot and humid, reminding me of Houston, Texas. My new teammates made me feel welcome. Several players stayed in a nice apartment complex, with a refreshing pool. I know my son, Will, enjoyed a daily dip, and the wives had each other for company, while we went on a road trip.

Our manager, Whitey Blackburn, was somewhat of a character, along the lines of Casey Stengel. He was a good hitting instructor. I could have benefited from his teaching early in my career to curb my *pulling tendency*.

Don Pepper was our first baseman. His daughter, Dottie, became a star on the Ladies Professional Golf Tour. She currently is a television personality at Ladies Professional Golf tournament events.

Our second baseman, Dave Campbell, played in the major leagues and became a television announcer on major league networks.

Minor League Baseball has a history of promotions, designed to attract fans to the ballpark. Ticket prices, as well as food concession and program prices, are less expensive than at the major leagues. Promotions are geared to family fun and enjoyment. It would be remiss of me not to mention two individuals that I encountered many times throughout my career, Jackie Price and Max Patkin. These two men entertained young and older fans throughout the country.

Jackie Price performed prior to the start of the game. He had a cannon-like apparatus that shot a baseball to extreme heights. He jumped into his golf cart and attempted to catch the ball. I have *never* seen him miss! Sometimes, he would let our catcher try, and usually, he missed. In every case, the fans enjoyed Jackie's act.

Max Patkin, known as the "Clown Prince of Baseball," performed during the actual game. With hat on backward and a baggy uniform, he coached third base for a few innings. His pantomime antics and signals to "hold up" or "continue running" were comical and crowd pleasing. In one skit, with the pitcher and umpire's knowledge, he approached the batter's box with multiple bats and then fell amid the bats. Once in the batter's box, the pitcher would wind up and throw a *resin* bag! Max would suit up in the home team's clubhouse. There, we witnessed his fatigue after the exhausting work he endured in his act, usually in hot, humid summer weather in southern towns. He was a limber-jointed individual, and when some of us met him at a local club in the evening, we marveled at his moves on the dance floor.

Reflecting on Max Patkin reminds me of another famous performer, Eddie Feigner. Eddie was sometimes called "The Clown Prince of *Softball*." Unlike Max, Eddie's act was serious and featured enormous baseball talent. Eddie was a pitcher, who had formed a group called "The King and His Court." His team consisted of Eddie (the pitcher), a catcher, a first baseman, and a shortstop. His team took on all challengers. They rarely lost a game. Some clocked his pitches at 104 miles per hour! At times, he pitched blindfolded, pitch from second base, and throw behind his back. Strikeouts were common.

My personal contact with Eddie took place in a spring training game. The Yankees at one point had two AAA teams, Richmond and Denver. I played for Richmond, and Eddie tried to gain a spot on the Denver roster, putting softball on hold for this hardball venture. It was very weird facing a pitcher with a *complete* underhand delivery. The pitch came in fast, and he had a sinker and riser in his repertoire. I fouled off a few balls and eventually walked. It seemed like a great accomplishment.

I learned later that Eddie had trouble controlling the hardball vs his impeccable control of the softball. Don't weep for Eddie, however. He made millions, barnstorming all over the world, and became very famous. I thank Danny Whelan, a member of our golfing group for bringing up Eddie's name in a softball discussion. Danny was a good pitcher, athlete, and teammate in my high school days.

Recently, I was talking to my friend Al Harris about Eddie Feigner. Al was a legendary fast-pitch softball player in South Jersey in the 1960s and 70s. His personal experience and insight, together with physics, sheds some light on Eddie's plight. Al says the larger softball, with larger stitches, was easier to control and make the ball rise and sink. The distance between home plate and the pitcher's mound is 46 feet in softball and 60 feet 6 inches in hardball. Throwing a hardball with an underhand delivery from a longer distance requires a major adjustment. Nice try, Eddie!

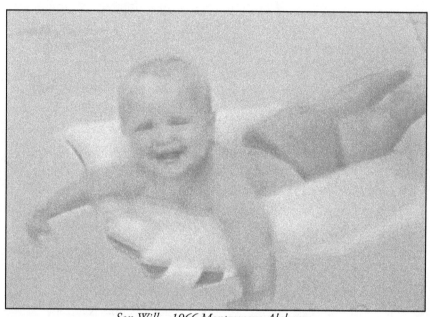

Son Will – 1966 Montgomery, Alabama

EXTRA INNINGS, BOTTOM OF THE TENTH:
Montgomery, Alabama

In the spring of 1966, I trained with Syracuse, New York, Detroit's AAA team. Even though I had started with one of the best and most difficult organizations, the New York Yankees, to advance to the top, other factors began to become a reality. Each new organization had their own young prospects, making it difficult to supplant them. So, I went back to Montgomery. Retirement became a serious consideration. My career and ultimate dream was coming to an end.

It's been said that if you are thinking about retirement, you are retired. However, your competitive spirit overcomes negative thoughts. Not completing the season was not an option. After much thought, I chose to retire at the end of the season. It was on my own terms of which I'm very proud. Many players receive releases early in their careers, some after a year or two. I was lucky to have enjoyed an eleven-year career. In retrospect, I have no regrets.

I've been asked if the time went fast while playing. It really didn't. When you are young, you think what you are doing will last forever. However, in baseball or any sport, thirty is considered *old*. Young nineteen and twenty year olds actively compete for your job.

I have also been asked why I signed with the Yankees. The Yankees were the best, and when you are young, you believe you are good enough to make it with the best. If the Yankees didn't think I was a *top prospect*, they wouldn't have pursued me.

As I'm writing my recollections and unbelievable experiences, I can truly say that the pursuit of the dream was undeniably worthwhile. Not many baseball players, minor or major, had the varied experiences I've had. Baseball, music, historic political and racial events, outstanding cities, and iconic individuals accounted for those experiences.

Unexpectedly, a Neil Young DVD provided the inspiration to record my memories. Hopefully, other dreamers reading this book will find their inspiration and pursue their goals. It's well worth it!

CITINGS

https://en.wikipedia.org/wiki/Guy_Rodgers#media/File:Guy_Rodgers.jpg
Public Domain photo taken by en:Carl Van Vechten, photographer.

https://images.search.yahoo.com/search/images;_ylt=AwrB8qBeZndau
Bettman getty fidel castro b Havana baseball 1959 – Yahoo Image Search…

http://www.espn.com/mens-college-basketball/story/_/id/16545360/fo
Bettman/Getty Images Hal Lear Temple

https://upload.wikimedia.org/wikipedia/commons/e/3/Ryman_Auditorium

https://en.wikipedia.org/wiki/File:Ryman_stage.jpg
From wikipedia, the free encyclopedia

https://en.wikipedia.org/wiki/Sulphur_Dell#media/File:Sulphur_Dell
Public Domain

https://en.wikipedia.org/wiki/Pepper_Martin

https://en.m.wikipedia.org.Mile_High_Stadium

https://w.w.w.baseballreference.com Havana Sugar Kings

https://en.wikipedia.org/wiki/Casey_Stengel

Cheng, Victor. Chasing Dreams. Case Interviews. September 29, 2014.

Ward, B.J. – Interview. Phaedra Trethan. Courier Post, New Jersey. Sunday
September 25, 2016.

Louisiana Division/City Archives | New Orleans Public Library |
neworleanspubliclibrary.org | New Orleans Pelicans Infielders / Outfielders

INDEX

Stengel, Casey, B2, B4, T2, T4, T10

T
Talbot, Fred, B8
Tresh, Tom. B3
Tubbs, Ernest, T7

U

V
Verdi, Frank, T5

W
Wallace George, T10
Williams, Billy, T6
Williams, Ted, B4, T6

X

Y
Young, Neil, ST, B10

Z

SUPPLEMENTAL INDEX

CPSIA information can be obtained
at www.ICGtesting.com
Printed in the USA
BVHW07s1613070718
521037BV00001B/153/P

9 781681 112268